A Child's Book of Dog Body Language

With Pictures

Help Keep Children Safe

By Amber Richards

Table of Contents

Note to parents   1

Critical Basics   5

Dog Eyes   15

Dog Mouths and Posture   19

Dogs and Their Tails   25

Barking Dogs   31

Dog Bites   39

Living with Dogs   43

Note to parents

This book is intended to be read to a child by an adult. Hopefully it will trigger good conversation and help keep children safe from dog bites, as well as help build good relationships with dogs. Sometimes fear of the unknown is worse than equipping children with basic knowledge, especially in a non-threatening environment such as reading a book with a loved adult, and not in the present moment with a dog.

It may be helpful for a child who is perhaps fearful of dogs, although caution when reading should be used. It is a difficult balance to strike, equipping safety strategies and yet not teaching fear. Each child is at different stages and has different feelings and experiences about dogs. What might be perfect for one child might be the worst thing for another. You know your child best. Please read this book yourself before reading to a child. Skip the parts that might be too much for them, and add more where needed, including some of your own experiences.

It is important to learn about dogs, how to treat them and how to look at their body language to try to tell how they are feeling. Learning these things helps to keep children safe from unfriendly dogs, as well as helping children to have good friendships with other dogs, and knowing how to treat them correctly.

A Child's Book of Dog Body Language

Critical Basics

Dogs can be amazing animals and best friends. They are usually friendly and loyal. They needed to be treated well with proper food in the right amounts, fresh water, exercise, and a good and loving home with people.

Here are some basics first about how to treat a

dog in general, even if it's your own pet. First is

never to hit a dog or tease them in any way. If

a dog is eating, drinking water or sleeping, leave

them alone, this is not the time for them to play.

Some dogs get very cranky when this happens

and might bite, when normally they wouldn't.

Don't ever sit or jump on a dog. Try to keep

calm and talk in a normal voice, not jumping up

and down and screaming. To some dogs, this is

frightening, or they can get over-excited.

Never walk up to a strange dog and try to pet it. Some dogs don't like children or are afraid of them, and with a dog you don't know, you can't tell if they are one of those or not. Instead, ask the adult with you if it's ok to pet the dog. That adult can ask the dog's owner if it is all right or not.

When you go to pet a new dog, slowly put your hand out and let them sniff your hand so they can see you won't hurt them. Then, gently pet the dog. On his back is best at first. Don't touch a dog's eyes, mouth, ears, feet or tail, as many do not like to be touched there.

In some ways, dogs are not that different from people. Just like people make their emotions known to each other, dogs give us signs that they are upset, angry, happy, or scared.

The problem is, we may not always be able to read dogs' emotions that well. We don't always get to learn about a dog's body language with pictures at school. A lot of people look at dogs' faces and think that they're always happy because they look like they're smiling!

Dogs have jaws that are shaped like a smile, but they express happiness in different ways. When we work with other animals, we have to remember that animals behave differently than we do, whether they are happy or sad.

When it's the family dog, it can be easier to know the dog's moods. You probably know your own dog better than a stranger's dog. You'll get to know him or her just like you would another friend. You may know when your dog is feeling happy, nervous, playful, or angry. Dogs bond with their human friends, too.

When it comes to paying close attention to what dogs do with their faces and bodies, in order to help keep children safe, it's even more important to do that with a strange dog than with your dog. Even beloved family pets can do things that are hard to plan ahead at times, so it's important to learn some basics about reading a dog's body language.

Understanding dogs' feelings can help you bond with your dog better, in addition to helping keep children safe. Dog behavior may seem strange to us, since they communicate with things we don't even have, like tails! There's a reason dogs do the things they do, and understanding those reasons can help humans and dogs of all ages live together.

When a dog is standing up on their hind legs,

the dog is begging or wanting something, usually

food. They are most likely friendly like this.

Another position that is usually friendly is when

a dog lies down on his back with his belly in the air. That is something called a submissive position, and they frequently want a new friend when they are in this position.

Dog Eyes

Sometimes, dogs do express themselves in a way that people can understand. When you or I feel just fine, our eyes don't usually do anything weird. It's the same thing with dogs.

When we get scared, our eyes will usually get big. It's the same thing for dogs. A dog with big, bulging eyes could be scared of anything, including you! Sometimes, dogs can do scary things when they are afraid, so it is better to try to wait for a scared dog to calm down, or avoid him or her entirely. Dogs can look squinty when they are scared as well, but they also might be sick.

As with a lot of other things, it's best if dogs don't make their eyes too big or too small; the middle is just right.

When your dog is at home and he or she has a favorite toy, it is sometimes best not to try to take it away. You might go up to your dog, and he or she won't face you, but the dog will still seem to be looking at you anyway. At that point, you'll probably see the white part of the dog's eyes. Usually, that means the dog means business, and it is better to back away from him or her.

In the wild, the ancestors of dogs would worry about other animals and other dogs taking their food away. Today, a lot of dogs still have that same fear, which they inherited from wild dogs, and they don't even know it. This is called instinct. Some dogs don't mind as much and can share their toys easily, which is why it is important to learn how to read them.

Dog Mouths and Posture

Happy dogs may open their mouths a little or keep them shut. Dogs can't sweat like people can (which is one way people can cool off), so a peaceful dog with an open mouth might just be feeling too hot, this is called panting.

When dogs are angry, one of the first places you notice it is on their mouths. They show their sharp front teeth, and their noses get wrinkly. Usually, they'll also growl at the same time. Dogs are showing you their teeth like that to make you back off, and it's usually a way to warn you, but if you see a dog doing this, it is very important to slowly back away. Do not turn your back and run. Try practicing this with an adult and perhaps a stuffed toy. Never go towards or try to pet a dog that is doing this.

Dogs can show their teeth for lots of reasons.

They will show their teeth while yawning.

Sometimes, they'll keep their heads down and

squint, but they'll still show lots of teeth. Usually,

dogs are just being friendly and humble when

that happens.

Their posture says it all: angry dogs look tense and stiff, with their heads high. Dogs that are keeping their heads to the ground and standing low and lazily probably aren't angry. Scared dogs almost look like they're trying to shrink!

Happy dogs look normal: we usually imagine

dogs looking that way.

Sometimes, angry dogs will have their fur

standing up, too (this is called getting their

hackles up). It will usually be the fur on their

back and the back of their necks that stands up

as a warning sign to back away immediately. It can be easier to see on some dog breeds than others: some dogs look like all of their fur is standing up all the time! Dog fur is just another piece of the puzzle for reading dogs.

Dogs and Their Tails

Anyone who's ever had a dog knows how much dogs wag their tails! They always look so happy, and we usually think they're happy if they're wagging their tails at us. Sometimes, though, happy dogs don't wag their tails. Dog tails can look so different that reading them can be strange!

Happy dogs will wag their tails from one side to the other, but their tails won't be sticking up and they won't be tucked in at all. Scared dogs will lower their tails, but their tails may still move like they did during happier times. Dogs will wag their tails more quickly depending on how strong their feelings are: happy dogs will wag their tails very quickly, and scared dogs might do the same thing.

Angry dogs will have their tails sticking out and probably curling up too, although they may still wag them. Dogs who keep their tails still while their tails are standing up could also be feeling angry: a dog holding his or her tail up is a sign that the dog thinks something is wrong.

Some dogs that do this with their tails may only be concentrating on something. If you ever walk your dogs and they see a squirrel, you'll usually see their tails go up, even though their bodies won't change otherwise. Their ears might stick up when they're concentrating on something, unless their ears always look like that.

Dog ears aren't as expressive, since there's only so much you can do with them, but dogs that are feeling easygoing will just have ears in a normal position. This dog with his ears slightly forward and head tilted shows that he is extremely curious and interested in something.

With dogs, you have to look at the whole picture sometimes. Even their tails give us clues to how a dog is feeling.

Barking Dogs

Dogs communicate by barking, it's their way of talking. They can bark for all sorts of reasons. Yelping usually means the dog is feeling scared or humble, not angry. If the rest of their body language says that they're happy or relaxed, there's no reason to worry. Sometimes they bark when they are lonely, an sometimes when they are feeling playful.

Angry barking tends to be faster and louder than

normal barking, although it can all sound strange

to people. A dog that looks angry in other ways will probably bark in a way that is more forceful than a normal bark. Angry barking dogs are trying to drive threats away by looking and sounding scary.

Angry dogs can look very scary from the outside. Fortunately, dogs do not usually get angry for no reason at all. Knowing that, we can try to work with them. When you learn about a dog's body language with pictures and practice in real life, learning the right thing to do and what NOT to do with a dog that is very clearly angry, you can help keep yourself safe.

Angry dogs are usually trying to protect what they think is their territory. When their backs arch and they growl at you, they're trying to warn you not to come closer. They don't know what you're going to do, and they're just trying to keep you away from them.

When you see a dog that looks really angry like that, the most important thing to do is not to look the dog directly in the eye. Dogs might think that you pose a threat; in a way, they'll think you're inviting them to a fight, because that's the way dogs behave towards each other.

Your dog at home might look you in the eye sometimes, because happy, friendly dogs are used to playing with humans and they know that looking them in the eye is okay. A strange dog may not have grown up the same way your dog did. He or she may be used to being a guard dog that gets into fights all the time. When a dog is already obviously angry, looking them in the eye can make the problem worse, even with a dog that is normally friendly.

Another important thing to remember is not to run away from the angry dog. It seems hard to believe. Running away seems like the most natural thing to do, and you might feel scared and want to run away. Dogs are very fast though, no matter how fast you are, and angry dogs will be faster than you. They also have a strong instinct to chase something that's running away.

Running away from an angry dog tells them that you're prey and they need to catch you. The best thing to do when facing an angry dog is back away very slowly. When you are far enough away from the dog, you can relax and move on, since he or she probably won't follow you then.

Talking to the dog may seem like the most natural thing to do, since that's what we do with people who misunderstand us. The dog is just going to see that as you threatening him or her; you'll be talking, but the dog will hear a bark. Finding an angry dog is scary, but yelling at the dog is definitely no good, no matter how scared you feel.

If you back away slowly from the dog without looking him or her in the eye, the angry dog will think that he or she has won the battle. Really, though, you both won!

Dog Bites

If all else fails and a dog tries to bite you, grab something else and thrust it at the dog. If you have a backpack, for instance, try to move it so he or she will bite that instead of you. Try to keep your body away from the dog's mouth as much as possible.

The dog might keep going or not. If that happens, yell for help, and yell loudly, keep yelling until someone helps you. Someone in the neighborhood might own the dog or know how to handle dogs. There's no shame in calling for help.

If you find yourself down on the ground with a dog trying to bite you, curl yourself tightly into a ball and cover your face and head with your arms. Keep yelling for help. Practice this position with an adult.

Dog bites can be very scary, but fortunately, there is a lot that we can do for them today. After getting bitten by a dog, get an adult to help you. Washing the dog bite with soap and water makes it less likely that you will get sick.

When it comes to dog bites and other kinds of bites, it depends on how bad the bite is. Some bites are so light that you can barely see them. All you have to do with them is give them a rinse with warm water and soap. Then, you can put some antibiotic cream on the bite. That way, it won't swell up and hurt!

You might have to go see a doctor if the bite from the dog was really bad, and there can be a lot of blood when a bite goes really deep into the skin. If you take a clean towel and press hard on the bite for a while, the bleeding will start to slow down and stop.

Always tell a parent or a trusted adult if a dog or any other animal bites you. They'll know what to do, and they can help you feel better. Lots of people get dog bites, and they're fine – the important thing is taking care of them properly.

Living with Dogs

Some dogs are more aggressive than others. Usually, it just depends on the individual dog. Some breeds of dogs were bred to be guard dogs, so they are more likely to get angry. Other dogs were trained to be that way.

People will usually choose dog breeds based on what they want from the dogs. Someone who wants a family dog might get a Golden Retriever or a breed that has a good reputation as a family dog, and will raise the dog to be friendly and good with kids. Someone who wants a hunting dog might get a bloodhound or another dog that is known to have a good nose. Some dog breeds are bred for sheep herding, like Border Collies.

Someone who wants a guard dog might get a pit

bull, German Shepherd, Doberman, or a

Rottweiler.

Little dogs can leave mean bites too, just like

cats, so they should be watched as well.

However, knowing about dog body language can

help keep children safe.

Dogs are called 'man's best friend' for a reason,

and there's no reason to be afraid of most dogs

that you meet throughout your day. People may

walk their dogs in your neighborhood, or bring

dogs to school. You may go to the beach or the

park and see people walking their dogs and

letting them run and play. Many of your friends and relatives will have dogs, or they may get dogs one day. Your family may even decide to get a dog if they don't already have one, or you may want one of your own someday.

Some dogs are trained to help people who can't see (called blind) to walk safely around objects and to help keep their owners safe. Some dogs help rescue and find people in trouble, and some dogs are even police dogs!

If your family or friends have dogs, going with the dogs on walks and playing with them can help you feel more comfortable with the way dogs move and express themselves. Eventually, knowing a dog's body language will just come naturally, but as you are learning about it, the use of pictures of dogs can be helpful.

Here are a couple more pictures to make you smile.

Amber Richards

The End

If you enjoyed this book or received value from it in any way, would you be kind enough to leave a review for this book on Amazon? I would be so grateful. Thank you!

CPSIA information can be obtained at www.ICGtesting.com
Printed in the USA
LVIW01n1618161015
458586LV00002B/14

9 781503 353633